Theodore Sabo is a resident of Washington State and an extraordinary lecturer at North-West University of South Africa. He has published six books including *Origins of Eastern Christian Mysticism*.

Theodore Sabo

DREAMS

AUSTIN MACAULEY PUBLISHERS™
LONDON • CAMBRIDGE • NEW YORK • SHARJAH

A CIP catalogue record for this title is available from the British Library.

ISBN 9781035861019 (Paperback)
ISBN 9781035861026 (ePub e-book)

www.austinmacauley.com

First Published 2024
Austin Macauley Publishers Ltd®
1 Canada Square
Canary Wharf
London
E14 5AA

Table of Contents

Dreams

Spring

The lone composer scribbled down
Notes, right hand paralyzed. Icy
Xylophones guttered like candles.
White vistas stretched out endlessly.

Chinook from Siberia blew.
Dreams of a Byzantine dress rose.
For a princess violets bloomed.
Ophelia wrung out her clothes.

Lilacs dripped. Apple blossoms fell.
Paint on *View of Toledo* dried.
Eastward the magic carpet flew,
Whisking Aladdin and his bride.

To Pacific continents raced.
Seaside piers jutted. Arctic set.
Over the Tian Shan morning
Dawned lavender and violet.

The Flying Dutchman

The Dutchman plowed. Alaska dreamt.
White languorous Kundry slept.
Alabaster glowed. Olives stirred.
Continents dripped azure. Dawn wept.

The planets spun. Irises bloomed.
Babylon's Hanging Gardens blew.
Sahara glistened. Rainbows fell.
From turquoise Cinderella flew.

Arles shimmered: yellow, sensuous.
The candles guttered cyanide.
Verses of Captain Lebyadkin
Sorrowed. The little mermaid died.

Rapunzel lowered her tresses.
The ancient wonders rushed. Skies shook.
The moon fled, nocturnal and pink.
Stars swelled. *The Jungle Book* awoke.

Scheherazade

Breezes from the cypresses blew.
Seas slept, African brides. Flowers
Trickled. The Gulf current blossomed.
Russian nights stole August showers.

In the pale sky the crescent moon
Swelled lavender. Tears became dawn.
Last wild poppies glistened. Stars swirled.
Maroon and blue Babylon raced.

Alluring lilacs spawned cyclones.
Evenings spilled orange groves. The simoom
Brought damasked Lady Godivas.
Time, an azure colossus, sped.

Seacoasts shuddered. Love the sorceress
Ran. Dew dripped budding cherry trees.
Afternoon, robber of hazel,
Dozed. The Chinese nightingale died.

Dawn

Alaska plowed. An Eskimo
Girl gathered berries of the night.
The moon turned on. Orion laid
His belt on an ocean of light.

Dawn vomited Arctic flowers.
Sacagawea glowed. Blue hills
Became hurricanes. Snowstorms
Fell in love with the windowsills.

Comets above the continent
Raced. The mistral blew canvases.
Horizons lagged far behind
Azure cyclones. Cézanne was born.

Simoom buried lilac planets.
The desert bred cancerous stars.
Smoke gutted the western expanse.
Apple trees soared endlessly.

April

April slept. Clumsy snowstorms raged.
Lilac nights fled. Comets swam.
Pacific chinook blew. Ingrid's
Lament blossomed. Anitra whirled.

Winter, lover of stars, scudded.
The centuries stumbled and fell.
Lamps on roofs burned. Seas swirled violet.
Smudge pots gutted painters' canvases.

The new planet throbbed. Galaxies
Spun. Alaska glowed: fiery,
Rose-faced. Arctic winds, Eskimo
Dreams, flew. The hurricane arose.

The Idiot

The moon stood over Moscow like
A guardian angel. Amber
And pink Aglaya dreamed.
The Annunciation darkened.

El Greco slept in a lilac dawn.
Women with mango blossoms flew.
Streams drank laburnum petals. Winter
Dug white trenches. Monsoon blew.

Azure gave birth to new candles.
Daffodils withered. Night enslaved
Periwinkle clouds. Rogozhin's
Shadow froze. The Chinese vase broke.

Klimt

Snow fell on distant Pluto.
Roger and Angelica loomed.
After seacoasts the stars lusted.
The colossus of Rhodes crumbled.

The typhoon spun. Orange groves hurried.
Footprints oozed. Contrails shook the skies.
Aquamarine Tahiti drowned.
Lilacs vomited butterflies.

Northern dawns rushed. Ukraine thawed.
The silver dove brought April winds.
Feast in the house of Simon rose.
Canoe rides became magenta.

Before icons candles fluttered.
Dazed, the jack of diamonds fled.
Lightning flashed. Blue horizons raced.
The stars, azure violets, swam.

Dostoevsky

Red fishes drove in a pink dawn.
The yellow cow sauntered. Tower
Of Pisa leaned. Roman candles
Budded. Violette Heymann dozed.

Storms covered drowsy seacoasts.
Ice from far Siberia formed.
Kafka's *Castle* glowed. Lighthouses
Fell into constellations.

The Japanese current scudded.
Flowers spawned Indonesian girls.
Branches against windowpanes bloomed.
Purple Torre del Lago sped.

Island maidens through the air ran.
The colossus shivered and froze.
Lavender swooned. Snow flew from clouds.
Brangäne's love potion soared.

November

Queen of scarlet wore a golden
Necklace. Arctic the fireman
Quenched burning trees. On Hans Brinker
Lakes the pink Netherlands skated.

November marigolds dampened.
Before Herod the stars, winter's
Sisters, danced. The Magi rode
On gingerbread horses.

Vancouver like a cherry tree
Blossomed. Apollinaire fell in love.
The chestnut-colored woman
Dreamed of lavender bedrooms.

Over red maples the wind flew.
Turquoise gave birth to black rams.
Milky Way, the charcoal burner's
Daughter, wove Cinderella stories.

Pelleas and Melisande

Sinewy clouds flew overhead.
October dropped aureate leaves.
Sunsets hatched Tivoli Gardens.
On cherry blossoms moonlight fawned.

Trains turned into cyclones.
The ocean played a Celtic harp.
Blinds lowered. The coastline darkened.
Seagulls flirted with the stern scarp.

Juneau blew. At Cana wedding
Feasts became drunk. Mornings bathed dark
Chrysanthemums. Amber pictures
Stretched out against magenta skies.

Christmas read Byzantine novels.
Lilac midnights fell asleep.
Lattices leaned. Silver lamps glowed.
Potudan River ran its course.

Birthday

Comets flashed. Dark azure stumbled.
To Bluebeard husbands vanilla girls
Spun Arabian legends.
Picasso soared. Lilac rooms dampened.

Snowflakes danced. Rouen Cathedral flamed.
Stars watched amber-haired
Princesses. Lanz of Salzburg died.
Childhood of Frederick the Great opened.

Jetties pointed eastward. From walls
Plaster dripped. The moon, drunk on
Cowboy songs, chased lavender nights.
April oceans spewed driftwood.

The Tempest

Arizona swooned under snows.
Pink clouds floated on turquoise skies.
Art deco girls spun fishing nets.
Hateful of the sea Caliban raged.

Zothar walked on slender knees.
Petals dripped fire. The West came apart.
Evenings flamed. Through white windows
The sweet papaya stole.

Under moonlit hills storms sank.
The dark-tressed goddesses bathed.
Tides surged, purple sand underfoot.
Nights oozed lilac trees.

Ocean foam dazzled. Stars fell asleep.
The blue-dark wind arose. Enchantress
Of the red slip slumbered.
Azure eyes of Miranda shone.

Summer

Wuthering Heights burst into storm.
Blue-pink Desdemona's
Willow song became pregnant.
Tulips danced under windmills.

Rain wrecked Picasso's dreams.
Cyclones discoursed with the night.
Behind churning topaz
Gardenia blossoms hung.

At dawn the whirlwind died.
The apricot vase fell into shards.
Peach trees faded. Lilac phantoms
Kissed azure windowsills.

Kandinsky

Easter eggs flew away.
Spring turned caramel and butterscotch.
On violet afternoons
Rikke Holst planted snowdrops.

Greek texts lay opened.
April caressed curtainless windows.
Ladybugs clung to love letters.
Dante finished *Purgatory*.

Aquamarine waves with coral
Blistered. Seas rained down
Geranium petals. Winter
Fell asleep from lullabies.

Snow-white day darkened. Azure,
Befriender of comets, set.
Under neon lights Thai harlots
Moved. Gold and red pagodas gleamed.

Pocahontas

Tuscan maids gathered peonies.
Pinturicchio drew
Apricot leaves. Lucrezia
Ran on silver feet.

Summer wore almond dresses.
Noon, lover of seals, sprouted
Orange blossoms. Pineapples fell into
The laps of Tahitian infants.

Shostakovich appeared before
Jazz combos. Night storms broke.
Moonlight scattered rice candy.
Clown's purple aubade began.

Indian Summer

October painted gray squares.
Shepherdess of lemon peels ripened.
Pacific sands abducted
Girls stained with wheat, enemies of Spring.

In love with cicadas
Princesses climbed laurel branches.
Eskimo whirlwinds overdosed
On lavender clouds.

Bronze parakeets glistened.
The Alps shone orange and crimson.
Courtesans lost wedding rings
In hyacinth pools.

Night

Texas gathered night's pale rays.
The moon's bridegroom addressed
The commendatore in Spanish.
Linda Isolde combed her hair.

Among revelers Lucrezia
Appeared. Mulberry feasts embarked
From green castles. White flowers
Brought winter to Verona.

From jeweled smithies Alps
Were drawn out golden and pink.
Count Almaviva flung
His pack of cards against the sky.

December Laos of roses
Drew Pinturicchio memories.
Queen of the wind stole dresses
From the white knight's maidens.

Renaissance Europe

Cape Verde snored under drunken tides.
Vespucci watched clear sands
Of New Mexico. Cloud daughter
Outran indigo hurricanes.

The Minoan games turned ivory.
Petals unspooled from lavender boughs.
Milk-colored dryads
Saw Zagreus in the forest.

To Constantinople Prester John
Sent gifts of labdanum.
Stewardess of Tahiti
Caressed the dying sailor.

Atalanta's feet raced
Over sharp shingle.
Unafraid of rain, aster girls
Sang gallows songs.

September

Snowboarders rode on Arctic stars.
Blue storms ransacked Dante's room.
The diseased captain copied maps
Of the West Indies.

Wisteria bloomed. Ultramarine
Cats told stories of Samoa.
Raspberry Esmeralda
Prayed for magenta rain.

The silver horse made tracks
For Portugal.
Childe Harold stole
Inés de Castro's alabaster jar.

Titian mixed paints for Venus
Of Urbino. Olive trees
Sprouted gold miniskirts:
Palomino leaves.

Boccaccio

The magenta princess led
Agathos over red sands.
September brushed Lavinia's
Peony tresses.

Blackbeard's ship came apart
Over reefs of coral.
Under the Japanese apple tree
Auburn Leda's night began.

Brown sibyls sat in lilac mines.
Roses drank spiced poison.
Naomi on the water tower
Stripped yellow bananas.

Rapids broke under Lohengrin's horse.
Wizard of false spring scared away
The gray-eyed shepherdess.
Snowflakes memorized diaries of Paul Klee.

The Cider Feast

Copper stars stood out against
Hyacinth skies. Distant cities shone.
Mistress of fallen leaves
Ascended diamond stairs.

Arctic painted from live models.
Daphne burst into flower.
Envious of banyans, magical
Islands plundered aloe baths.

Topaz laughed at the messenger
Of the czars. Green mirrors
Sent raspberry wine
To Baudelaire's mulattoes.

King Christian II

Lemon rings dripped.
Geranium petals
Bent seaside windows.
Through autumn hazel slept.

The star whirlwind lifted.
Whortleberries blushed.
Tom Bombadil outwitted
Shoshone river brides.

Spring wheels became mushrooms.
Dawn ate sugar plums.
Wild swans rescued Prince Myshkin
From vanilla prisons.

Pinturicchio

Boreal winds fetched rhododendrons
From Alaska. October lugged
Cherry boxes up apartment stairs.
Blondes in pink kissed tramps under bridges.

Schlesinger's Italy fled
In train cars. Towns on hills
Reflected tanned gardens. Autumn
Searched for Edain's blouse in sunlit rooms.

Red maples dried. Samoans
Led Klimt to ivory brothels.
Midnight dawned in Solomon's palace.
On gray couches Queen of Sheba lay.

Geese flew above the maroon wood.
Blackbirds swayed in gypsy branches.
Dublin policemen befriended
Juliet by the drinking fountain.

March

March dripped. Linda Isolde
Leaned from her window.
Under clothesline Tasso
Dug enchanted gardens.

Telemachus lit his electronic
Hookah. Space frogs pursued
Amber-tressed Neaera
With laser blasters.

Like Viking ships orange birds
Alighted on auburn wells.
Golden-skinned Isolde
Passed through sunlit trellises.

Birch trees scrubbed lilac-gray clouds.
Samantha Nausicaa and her dalmatians
Watched Humpty Dumpty
On the flying trapeze.

Towards Africa

Valentinus

I watched. The long spacious day slipped through my fingers.
There were women like obsidian in smoothness;
There were merchants balancing their coins on golden scales;
There were philosophers with their pupils and scholars
With their books of learning. But best of all was a child
Who called me by my name and told me all I knew
Of Silence and Depth, of Father and Forefather,
Of Wisdom and Redeemer, of God and Man.

A Biblical Dancer

A dancer dances in Samian red
Before a drunken prince and his nobles.
The prince can no more plumb the whims of her head

Than tell why the insensible rain falls
Nightlong on the roofs, or why golden kings
Wind their tortuous way through hermetic halls,

Calculating the murderous things
That will bring new guests to the courts of the dead:
A martyred girl who seemed a bird with wings,

A fugitive and his purloined royal bride
Whose beauty was like the summer sun's rising,
A coarse-girt prophet who quickened his end

By his mockery of a petty king
And stirred up his queen to a madcap hatred,
Throwing to the winds his meager following.

A dancer dances in Samian red,
A luminous creature, no brood of chance,
And the insensible rain falls overhead

To keep her ignorant of all but her dance.

Towards Africa

I fix a sail towards Africa, my boat
In the shape of a dhow. I have set out
From the east in midsummer and passed seas
Glutted with stonefish dwelling off oases
Engirt with stone and pebble and mallee leaf
And shrubbery sacred to Adam and Eve.
I am tortured with unrest until I moor
At Africa's sheltered sunlit harbor.

Finding its enameled shore under my feet
I wind my way through an elaborate street
Thronged with black orient-attired shop women.
From here a Christian king sent gifts to lighten
Luxurious Constantinople's woes
And would have given more were not his foes,
The converts of a Bedouin prophet,
Setting his distant provinces alight.

In the courtyard the African leaves stirred;
All day the spray of a fountain jetted.
He mused on a throne surrounded by palms:
His fathers raised up those marble columns
And fashioned those walls of marble and gold,
Those gates of ruby, ivory, and emerald.
Why had he betrayed their pagan labors
For a faith that trampled the brute pleasures?

Was it because of his chivalrous creed
And the barbaric spirit it unmade
He knew no way to beat down the nomad hordes
Whose daily advance terrified his lords?
Today nothing remains of his palace
But the tortoises playing in their bliss,
The sun spilling out its golden luster,
Its rays mirrored by a vat of quicksilver.

Numberless realms have followed his to their doom,
Realms ruled by a king who murdered without qualm
A vassal who begged the hand of his sister,
Or a queen so stung by a prophet's ardor
She dreamed up his death by an ax's plunge.
There was no more poignant token of that age
Than the girl exiled with her to ancient France
Who hurtled her life away for a dance.

I too have charted these seas not to gain
A vision of a king's ruin, the turbaned plain,
The convoys that would crush his boyish hopes,
The sword he unsheathed to perish with his troops,
But to drink in his era's opulence
And glimpse those jetties paved with precious stones,
Where caravel on caravel unmoored
To dispense the bounty of an Eastern lord.

Prester John

He sits on his throne of ruby gold,
His scepter a single emerald.
He wonders whether he had been wise
To forsake his fathers' pleasantries
For a self-abasing religion;
At his gate hammers the barbarian.
Nothing he can do but beseech God
Tomorrow his race will not be dead:
He prays on his throne of ruby gold,
His scepter a single emerald.

Platonic Love

Amid wan flowers by a brook
A unicorn lies near a queen;
He pirouettes his neck to look
At her whose voice is sweet as wine.

Her furs and emblem of queenhood
Are studded with shards of silver;
They cover her from toe to head
Save for her face and before where

Her studded robe begins its slide.
The robe invests her body
With an odalisque's lassitude,
A wet swimmer's refulgency.

Insensible to her madcap youth,
To each scampering day and hour,
She has daubed on her willing mouth
Paint less dark than her hooded hair.

None can say why she dons her furs,
So passionless her royal mood,
Or why she has snubbed her suitors
In the strange chill of womanhood.

They praise her for her peaceful mien:
Amid wan flowers by a brook
Where the air is sweeter than wine
A queen and a unicorn speak.

Zarathustra and the Dancers

Their brightness comes and goes at whim,
They dance as lightly as they can;
Although they are the wards of thieves
They seem the daughters of the sun.
One's face is a shimmering pool,
Another's hair a trailing vine;
All are white as carven ivory
And fragrant with myrrh and vervain.

Nietzsche

Say whatever you will, I hate
With an unappeasable hate
The fathers enslaving the sons:
Parsifal caught in the same noose
By Amfortas and Gurnemanz
Until he severed himself loose
And blessed them in a vernal wood
In the name of the three-personed God.

Idealism

Seven volumes of Velikovsky
Rest on my shelves, fragrant with spikenard.
Near them, like a cruel-eyed bird of prey,
A book of mythology stands guard.

The Apocalypse

When the Caesars' crowns sat heavy on them
And Thaïs suspired in religious gloom,
When Plotinus' mind mythicized Plato's,
Men thought the four angels had been set loose.

Political Chaos

Coligny dreamed up the murder
Of the duke of Guise—musket or sword
It mattered little—but never learned
The bitter harvest that he sowed.

To a Young Singer

Keep a child's simple heart in a grownup's body
And if fortune turns fickle count yourself lucky.
Rousseau if he knew the prospect of his future strife
Would never have abandoned the copyist's life
And Petrarch wished he'd spurned the poet's laurel crown
And died ignorant of popish leer and priestly frown.

Africa

East or west lies a continent battered
By the winds of war, disease, famine, and flood—
But trees put forth their leaves in February
Above a wide and circuitous river;
The natives wear clothes like the Magi wore
When they gave their Lord gifts of gold and myrrh;
A Kinshasa girl, spring's epitome,
Holds in her hand the blossom of a lily.

What do we not owe that tortured continent:
Jeweled animals set in their golden home,
The fabled mist-shrouded Ruwenzori,
Burton and Speke passing speckled shrubbery?
Last year I thought I could make a like journey
From Congo's thirty falls to Dar es Salaam,
But I was enslaved by a prose poem
About a Welsh king's world of bewitchment.

Beauty means something more to the African
Than it does to Asian or European.
His kinsmen no longer worship pagan gods,
But his young men still learn to sharpen spearheads,
His Granias to pass the narcotic cup
Among their guests, waiting for the fall of sleep
And after that the hurried flight through the woods,
A moonlit tree projecting its eerie shape.

If I were a believer in symbols
Their love would be a symbol of my desire,
Their thatched houses a symbol of my house
Where I would live not as the adventurer
Hoping to gaze on Victoria's brightness,
But as the Masai tribesman who undergoes
Arduous rites to become a warrior
And take his place in the throng of higher souls.

Cathar Girl

The smell of roots deep underground,
The region her body will lie,
Even the tendons of her left hand,
The creation of an ignorant god:
Like the God of the Old Testament
But with a black cloak and a staff like a Swiss pike,
Grasping it with dirty fingernails,
Wandering alone and discontented
By brambles of the desert and the pebbly streams.

Yet her gold hair, gold as the fulcrum of heaven,
Does not that overmaster you,
And the dark inscrutable eyelids?

Printed in the USA
CPSIA information can be obtained
at www.ICGtesting.com
LVHW012318260424
778567LV00006B/206